US AIR POWER

Modern Air Superiority Planes

US Marine Corps F/A-18C Hornet multi-role fighters from VMFA-212. This Marine unit is flying from Kaneohe Marine Corps Air Base in Hawaii, at the time of Operation 'Desert Shield' in 1990.

US AIR POWER

Modern Air Superiority Planes

Aircraft, Weapons and their Battlefield Might

Anthony A. Evans

Greenhill Books
LONDON

Stackpole Books
PENNSYLVANIA

Greenhill Books

Modern Air Superiority Planes: Aircraft, Weapons and their Battlefield Might
first published 2004 by Greenhill Books,
Lionel Leventhal Limited, Park House, 1 Russell Gardens,
London NW11 9NN
www.greenhillbooks.com
and
Stackpole Books, 5067 Ritter Road, Mechanicsburg,
PA 17055, USA

British Library Cataloguing in Publication Data

Evans, Anthony A.
Modern Air Superiority Planes. – (US air power: the
illustrated history of American air power, the campaigns,
the aircraft and the men)
1. United States. Air Force – Equipment and supplies
2. Air power – United States
3. Fighter planes – United States
4. United States – History, Military – 20th century
I. Titles
358.4'00973'09049

ISBN 1-85367-593-8

Library of Congress Cataloging-in-Publication Data available
The photographs in this book are courtesy of the United
States Department of Defense, the United States Air
Force, the United States Navy and the United States
Marine Corps.

Designed by DAG Publications Ltd
Design by David Gibbons
Layout by Anthony A. Evans
Edited by Hugh Schoenemann
Printed in Singapore

US AIR POWER
MODERN AIR SUPERIORITY PLANES

th more than 50 aerial kills over Iraq, the diterranean and in the skies over the Balkans, d with only one plane lost to enemy jet hters, modern US air superiority aircraft have unmatched combat record. The F-14 Tomcat, e F-15 Eagle, the F-16 Fighting Falcon, and the 8 Hornet and their pilots, have all shown eir unrivalled prowess when it comes to taking the foes of the US. The Tomcat gained its first ls back in 1981 when two US Navy aircraft ot down two Libyan Sukhoi Su-22s over the lf of Sirte in the Mediterranean. The others gan to notch up their victories over the bsequent decades.

Todays air superiority planes are the scendants of the 'pursuit' or 'fighter' planes the two World Wars. Their job was simply to oot down enemy aircraft. With the coming of e jet age the term 'fighter' became more mmonly replaced by the term 'intercepter', d today, 'air superiority'. But whatever they e called it all adds up to the same thing: ooting down enemy warplanes.

All have a formidable arsenal of missiles on ich they can call. As well as their powerful lti-barrelled Vulcan cannon, they have the est version of the Sidewinder heat-seeking ssile, and the 'fire and forget' Advanced dium Range Air-to-Air Missile (AMRAAM) vanced generation of missiles. The technology these supersonic aircraft – already superior to st other planes – is ever being improved, giving em an advantage over anything that dares to against them. These superb machines have performed magnificently for the US armed rces and will continue to do so in the future.

The most elderly is the Grumman F-14 Tomcat that was designed to replace the F-4 Phantom as a fleet air defense fighter. The first Tomcat was flown on December 12, 1970, with 556 aircraft starting to be delivered from 1972. Although primarily an air superiority fighter, it also can be configured for air-to-ground missions and has seen much action in that role over Iraq. Pre-revolutionary Iran has been the only export customer for the Tomcat with 79 being delivered.

The McDonnell Douglas F-15 Eagle also replaced the F-4 Phantom in USAF service and is without doubt the pre-eminent air superiority fighter presently in service with the US. It took to the air on July 27, 1972, entering service in 1976. The Eagle is in service with Israel, Japan and Saudi Arabia. It has seen excellent combat service with both the US and the Israeli Air Forces. There is a long range strike fighter variant, the F-15E.

The Lockheed Martin F-16 Fighting Falcon evolved out of the lightweight fighter program and first flew on January 20, 1974. A highly successful design, it has been exported to more than a dozen countries. It is a truly multi-role fighter and has seen much combat service in its various roles, both with the USAF and foreign airforces.

The McDonnell Douglas F/A-18 Hornet is also a multi-role fighter and was also the product of the US lightweight fighter program, first flying on November 18, 1978. It is in service with both the US Navy and the Marines. It has been exported to seven different countries. The F/A-18E Super Hornet is a significantly larger and more capable variant and first flew on November 18, 1995.

The next generation of US air superiority fighters are the Lockheed F-22 Raptor and the F-35 Joint Strike Fighter. The F-22 first flew on September 29, 1997, and it should enter service with the USAF in 2004. The F-35 first took to the air on December 16, 2000 and is due to enter service in 2008 with the USAF, USN and USMC. Also, the British Royal Navy and Royal Air Force are to take some 150 as Britain has a ten per cent development partnership in the project. This multi-role fighter will have a short take-off and vertical landing variant as well as the more conventional version.

Today's fighters are dependant on what are called 'Force Multipliers', such as Airborne Warning and Control Systems (AWACS) aircraft that maintain control of the aerial battlefield, aerial tankers to keep the warplanes topped up with fuel, extending their range, and specialized electronic jamming aircraft, designed to confuse enemy detection and radar systems.

Actual air combat can be basically divided into two. Long or beyond visual range, and close-range or 'dogfighting'. The former is when superior technology plays the major part. The use of AWACS or ground control radar would detect and identify hostile warplanes at long range. This information would be fed to any friendly fighters in the vicinity, who could then be vectored to the appropriate interception course. Then, with the aid of their onboard systems and radars, they would target and attack the enemy planes with medium or long range missiles without possibly ever even seeing the enemy aircraft.

In the close combat scenario, despite all the technological advances, close-range jet fighting still boils down to basic piloting skills. Training teaches the fighter pilot manoeuvers which should enable them to defeat their opponents. The primary weapons for this kind of combat are the short-range heat-seeking Sidewinder missile and the Vulcan cannon. 'Dogfighting' is a fast, three-dimensional game of manoeuvre

and counter-manoeuver where each pilot trying to outwit his opponent in order correctly position himself for the kill, at t same time trying to avoid being killed. Many these techniques of maneuver date back World War One and apply just the same biplanes, held together by string and glue, as the hi-tech supersonic jets of today.

The Weapons

The AIM-9 Sidewinder has been in consta production since 1954 and, in its many mar has been involved in just about every air w since, as it has been widely exporte Development began in 1950 by a US Na ordnance team and it was first successfully t fired on September 11, 1953.

Cost-effective and simple, with only son twenty moving parts, the short-ran Sidewinder uses the heat-seeking principle f guidance. Firing the early Sidewinder w simple; by pointing the infra-red (IR) homi head of the missile at a heat source, such as t jet exhaust of the target aircraft, a low growl heard over the pilot's headset when the miss acquires the target. As the range is closed a the heat source becomes stronger, the growli sound becomes more strident. At t appropriate moment, the missile is fire homing in on the heat source. The early mode could only detect targets within a 5-degree co directly ahead of the weapon's nose, so t launch plane had to be pointing directly at t target. Later versions could gain a lock-on fro any angle. The first production version was t AIM-9B and the missile has been progressive upgraded ever since, the newest version bei the AIM-9X.

The first use of the AIM-9 was on Septemb 14, 1958, during a clash between some twen Communist Chinese MiG-15s and fourte Chinese Nationalist F-86 Sabers, which each h been armed with two Sidewinders. T Nationalists claimed four MiGs brought dov by the missile. The Sidewinder made its first combat debut with the US Navy in the skies ov Vietnam and then with the USAF, bringing dov

er 80 enemy aircraft during the course of that
r.

The AIM-7 Sparrow medium range air-to-air
ssile is a Semi-Active Radar Homing (SARH)
apon. Development dates back to the late
40s, with the first test firing in 1953. The
st models of the missile were 'beam riders';
the launch plane estabished a radar lock on
target aircraft, the missile would acquire the
lar beam with its onboard sensors, and the
arrow would ride the beam to the target.
er versions used continuous wave radar
mination; the missile uses its own on-board
eiver which homes in on the target's radar
lection generated when the launch aircraft
ints' the target with its radar, the launch
craft having to maintain a radar lock on the
get. First used operationally during the
tnam War, the first results were
appointing, but with improvements and
grades, results became better. During the
lf War of 1991, the Sparrow acquitted itself
ll. The variant then in use accounted for 25
the 42 enemy planes shot down. The AIM-7
s been widely exported and various overseas
velopments produced. The Sparrow is still in
vice with the US although it has largely been
laced by the AMRAAM. Production of the
arrow continues, with the AIM-7R the current
del and older models being upgraded to the
M-7P model.

The AIM-120 AMRAAM was developed to
lace the Sparrow. In the nose of the missile
he on-board active radar seeker that allows it
seek out targets independently. The missile
ll relies on the launch plane for initial
geting and mid-course guidance, but for the
al phase its own radar acquires the target
d the launch plane can then turn away to find
re targets and let the missile track and hit
target all by itself. The AIM-120 has a range
over 30 miles and the range of its on-board
lar is possibly at least six miles. This missile
s proved its ability in combat over the skies
the Balkans and Iraq.

The AIM-54 Phoenix long range air-to-air
ssile is only carried by the F-14 Tomcat. The
concept of an air-to-air missile with a range of
100 miles dates back to the 1950s. This big
Mach 5 missile has a launch weight of 1,021lbs
and carries a warhead weighing some 132lbs.
The first deliveries of the Phoenix were in
December 1970 and trials completed in 1972.
On November 22, 1973, an F-14 fired a full
complement of six missiles against six target
drones. Four missiles made direct hits or
passed within a lethal distance, activating the
missile proximity fuse. This is the only time the
F-14's 'Six-Shooting' capability has been
demonstrated. In the 1970s, the US Navy saw
the jet bomber with long-range stand-off
missiles as the primary air threat to its fleet.
The Phoenix missile was the answer. The C
model has an anti-missile capability and marks
a distinct increase in the weapon's capability
over the previous A and B variants. A few
Phoenix missiles were fired in anger by the USN
against Iraqi MiG-25s but with no confirmed
kills reported.

With the entry into service of guided and
homing missiles, it was assumed that the gun
was dead as far as air-to-air combat was
concerned, and new fighters tended to
dispense with it. During air combat over
Vietnam it was realised that the variable
performance of the then current variants of US
missiles needed some back-up, and therefore
cannon were re-introduced.

The General Electric Vulcan cannon became
the weapon of choice. The very reliable and
radically new 20mm M61A six-barrel Gatling-
type cannon was blessed with a phenomenal
rate of fire: 6,000 rounds per minute. By the end
of the Vietnam War the weapon had brought
down 32 communist MiGs. It has equipped two
generations of US fighters and will be installed
on the F-22 Raptor, the next generation.

Dogfights over the Mediterranean
On August 19, 1981, two US Navy F-14 Tomcats
from VF-41 began a Combat Air Patrol (CAP) off
the Libyan coast in the Mediterranean Sea. They
detected a radar contact heading for them.
which proved to be two Libyan Sukhoi Su-22

'Fitter' jet fighters. As the two Libyan aircraft tried to maneuver to an attack position on the tails of the Tomcats, the F-14s turned away. The four aircraft then positioned themselves for a head-to-head confrontation; one of the Su-22s fired an 'Atoll' heat-seaking missile, which failed to track and missed the US planes. The F-14s quickly managed to position themselves each on the tails of the Libyans as they suddenly broke formation. Each Tomcat firing a Sidewinder missile, both tracking perfectly, hitting, exploding and bringing down the two Su-22s. Both Libyans were seen to eject. The Tomcat had achieved its first air-to-air kills.

F-14s would claim further Libyan kills on January 19, 1989, as a US Navy exercise was underway in international waters off Libya. Two Tomcats from VF-32 were flying from the carrier USS *John F. Kennedy* when two Libyan MiG-23s took off from their base. The two F-14 crews immediately picked them up on their radar from more than 70 miles away and flew straight toward them. After alerting the Libyans that the Tomcats were monitoring them, the four aircraft went into a manoeuvring contest as each of the planes tried to get on their opponent's tail. When the Libyan fighters manoeuvring became increasingly reckless and more aggressive, instructions came from the carrier that the F-14s could employ weapons if threatened. The F-14 crews had to assume the worst. Two Sparrow missiles were fired by one F-14 at a range of over twelve miles as the MiGs turned again and headed straight for the Tomcats, but the missiles failed to lock on. A third Sparrow was fired and guided well, striking one of the MiGs and exploding, the pilot managing to eject. The F-14s managed to get onto the tail of the remaining MiG and it was brought down by a single Sidewinder. Again the Libyan pilot was able to eject. The US air crews each received the DFC.

Iraq
Operation 'Desert Storm' began on January 17, 1991. By the end of the first day, US aircraft had

brought down nine Iraqi warplanes. During t[...] war 42 air-to-air kills were claimed, 35 of the[...] by F-15s (plus two by a Saudi F-15). The F-1[...] Eagles dominated the battlefield. The US Na[...] complained that their lack of aerial kills was [...] down to the fact that the AWACS' USAF cre[...] rather partisan attitude, tended to favour US [...] F-15s when it came to vectoring fighters o[...] any suspected enemy aircraft. A US Navy F-[...] did gain one kill though, and two F/A-18s t[...] more. Two USAF A-10s also had one each. O[...] one US aircraft was lost to an enemy aircraft[...] prowling MiG-25 managed to bring down [...] F/A-18C.

While on Operation 'Southern Watch', the [...] Fly Zone over southern Iraq, a USAF F-16 s[...] down an Iraqi MiG-25 on December 27, 19[...] and a MiG-29 on February 28, 1993, both k[...] using AIM-120 AMRAAMs. Other aer[...] altercations have occurred since, with missi[...] being fired, but no kills being recorded.

During Operation 'Iraqi Freedom' in 2003, [...] Iraqi Air Force wisely did not put any of [...] aircraft up in a futile attempt to oppose t[...] allies, so there were no air kills.

The Balkans
In October 1992, the UN imposed a No Fly Zo[...] for military aircraft over Bosnia. But the warri[...] factions ignored the NFZ, and NATO aircr[...] began Operation 'Deny Flight' which saw [...] hour Combat Air Patrols (CAPs) in the sk[...] over the former Yugoslavia. Helicopters tend[...] to be the main aircraft used by the warri[...] sides, and fixed wing planes were rarely use[...] But on February 28, 1994, two USAF F-16[...] intercepted six Serbian Air Force Jastrebs wh[...] were bombing the town of Bugojno. One F-[...] brought down one Jastreb with an AIM-1[...] AMRAAM and another two with AIM-9s, and t[...] second F-16 shot down a fourth Jastreb with [...] AIM-9.

During the 1999 Operation 'Allied For[...] on March 24, F-15 Eagles brought down t[...] MiG-29s and again on March 26 another t[...] MiG-29s. On May 4, a USAF F-16C shot dow[...] Serbian MiG-29 after firing two AIM-120s.

An F-14A Tomcat fighter of VF-74 taxis past three Tomcats on the flight deck of the aircraft carrier USS *Saratoga* (CV 60) during Operation 'Desert Storm'. The aircraft all have their wings fully swept back for ease of stowage on the crowded flight-deck and also in the hangars of the aircraft carriers.

Above and below: The F-14 is a supersonic, twin-engine, variable-sweep wing, two-seater fighter, designed to attack and destroy enemy aircraft in all weather conditions. It can track up to 24 targets simultaneously with its powerful radar system and engage and attack up to six with its Phoenix AIM-54 missiles. Armament can also include the full range of current air-to-air missiles plus a 20mm Vulcan cannon.

Opposite page: An F-15C Eagle flies a patrol over the desert after the end of Operation 'Desert Storm'. The aircraft carries a mix of four AIM-9 Sidewinder missiles on its wing pylons and up to four AIM-7 Sparrow missiles beneath its fuselage.

Above: Two F-15C Eagles of the USAF 36th Tactical Fighter wing before they were deployed to Saudi Arabia for Operation 'Desert Storm'. They are armed with the standard combination of the period: four Sidewinder and four Sparrow missiles, plus they have their Vulcan cannon.

Below: USAF security police stand guard near a fully armed F-15C Eagle in Saudi Arabia. Without doubt the Eagle is the pre-eminent US fighter since the mid-1970s. The size of these aircraft can be appreciated when compared with the security policemen.

Opposite page: An F-16C/J Falcon from the 52nd Fighter Wing based at Spandahlem AB, Germany breaks away after refuelling from a Stratotanker on March 31, 1999 while patroling the skies over Kosovo during Operation 'Allied Force'. It is armed with four AIM-120C AMRAAM air-to-air missiles on the outboard stations for self protection and two HARM (Highspeed Anti-Radiation Missiles) on the inboard stations to suppress any anti-aircraft radar sites.

Top: An F-16 here armed with Sidewinder missiles. The aircraft has seen service with the Air National Guard (ANG) as well the USAF.

Above: Two United States Air Forces Europe F-16s fly in formation during a mission in support of NATO Operation 'Allied Force'. The F-16s are from the 510th Fighter Squadron, Aviano Air Base, Italy. The lead F-16 is a single seat F-16CG and is carrying a full air-to-air combat load including four AIM-120 missiles, drop tanks, and an electronic jamming pod, and has both a laser designating pod as well as a FLIR (Forward Looking Infrared) pod on the intake sides. The second F-16 is a F-16DG and is armed with two AIM-120 missiles on the wingtip station and two Sidewinders on the outer stations.

Above: An F/A-18C Hornet of Fighter Attack Squadron Eight One (VFA-81) during Operation 'Desert Shield'. VFA-81 was operating from the aircraft carrier USS *Saratoga*. The airplane is carrying an AIM-9 Sidewinder on each wingtip.

Below: Aboard USS *Theodore Roosevelt* (April 17, 1999), flight deck crewmembers prepare an F/A-18 Hornet for launch along the forward catapult. USS *Theodore Roosevelt* (CVN 71) and its embarked carrier air wing were participating in air strikes over the former Yugoslavia in support of NATO Operation 'Allied Force'.

Above: A US Navy F/A-18F Super Hornet on final approach to the deck of the aircraft carrier USS *John C. Stennis* (CVN 74) during the aircraft's initial sea trials in waters off the coast of North Carolina. The Super Hornet, the Navy's newest fighter aircraft, is the programmed replacement for the F-14 Tomcat.

Below: On board the aircraft carrier USS *America*, an F-14 Tomcat of Fighter Squadron One Zero Two (VF-102) about to launch from the catapult in January 1997. It is being passed by an F/A-18 of Fighter Attack Squadron Eight Six (VFA-86).

?ove: A Fighter Squadron Three Two (VF-32) – the 'Swordsmen' – F-14A Tomcat in the foreground flies alongside a ?antom II of the British Royal Air Force in 1990. The Tomcat replaced the Phantom in US Navy fighter service when the ?ter had been phased out of service in 1986. In 1983 during Operation 'Urgent Fury', the 'Swordsmen' flew air defence and ? superiority missions over Grenada. After that they proceeded to the Mediterranean aboard the USS *Independance* and ?w reconnaissance missions over Syrian military sites in Lebanon.

?ow: Two 'Swordsmen' F-14s went on to shoot down two Libyan MiG-23s in 1989 and the squadron went on to also play a ?ry important part in the Gulf War of 1991.

Above: An F-14 Tomcat aircraft receives pre-flight systems checks on catapult onboard the USS *Constellation* (CV 64), while conducting routine flight operations in support of Operation 'Southern Watch', April 14, 2001. The carrier's huge superstructure is visible in the background.

Below: A deck edge operator on a catapult looks away from the jet blast of an F-14A Tomcat as it is launched from the deck of the USS *Kitty Hawk* (CV 63). The F-14A is powered by two Pratt & Whitney TF30-P-412A/414 turbofans each rated at 20,900lb of thrust with afterburners.

Above: With a top speed of 1,544mph and an absolute service ceiling of 56,000ft, the Tomcat is still one of the most formidable intercepters in the world. This Tomcat is from the 'Gunfighters', Fighter Squadron One Two Four (VF-124), which operated the aircraft from October 1972 until September 1994 when the squadron was disestablished and its aircraft were transferred to other squadrons.

Below: A long-range Phoenix air-to-air missile being fired from an F-14. This Tomcat is from the 'Black Knight' squadron, Fighter Squadron One Five Four (VF-154), which started flying the aircraft from 1984 with a compliment of twelve fighters. The squadron was involved in Operation 'Desert Shield', but missed Operation 'Desert Storm'.

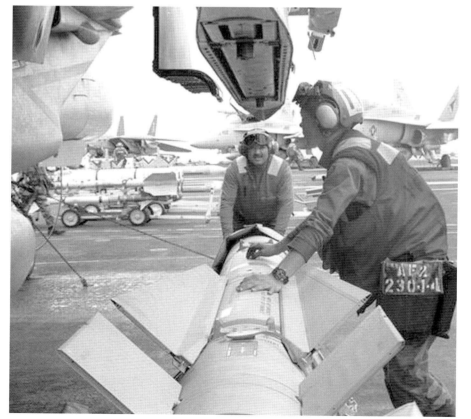

Above: A huge Phoenix air-to-air missile is wheeled across the flight deck prior to being loaded onto a Tomcat.

Left and top right: Aviation ordnancemen load an AIM-54C Phoenix missile onto an F-14B Tomcat wing and (top right) another one under the fuselage.

Below right: The Radar Intercept Officer (RIO) conducts a pre-flight inspection on a fuselage-mounted AIM-54C Phoenix air-to-air missile while aboard the aircraft carrier *Abraham Lincoln,* whose Battle Group was in the Persian Gulf in support of United Nations sanctions against Iraq.

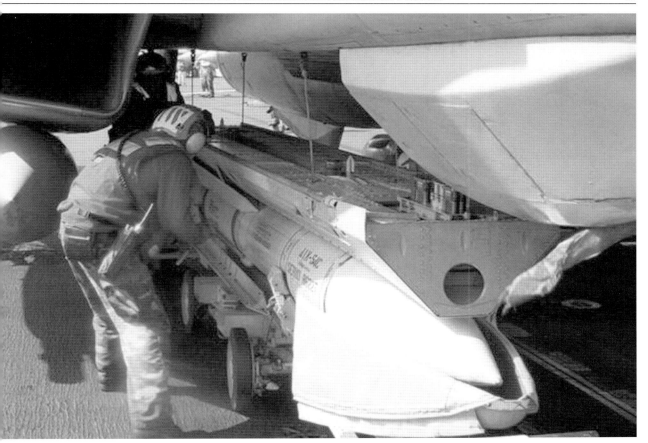

Left: Aboard USS *Enterprise* (CVN 65) November 9, 2001, F-14 Tomcats prepare to take off from the flight deck for a final time. This was the last time the aircraft would be deployed on the carrier. USS *Enterprise* then returned to her home port in Norfolk, Virginia after completing a regularly scheduled deployment.

Right: An aviation ordinance mate performs a post-flight check on an AIM-9 Sidewinder short-range air-to-air missile attached to an F-14 Tomcat assigned to the 'Bounty Hunters' Fighter Squadron Two (VF-2) in support of Operation 'Iraqi Freedom', the Persian Gulf (March 25, 2003).

Right: At sea aboard USS *Theodore Roosevelt* (CVN 71) in the Mediterranean, February 26, 2003, an F-14D Tomcat assigned to the 'Black Lions' of Fighter Squadron Two One Three (VF-213) is launched from one of four steam-powered catapults on the ship's flight deck.

Left: These three F-14A Tomcats fly in formation on their final approach to USS *Kitty Hawk* (CV 63) on April 3, 2003. The USS *Kitty Hawk* Carrier Strike Force and Carrier Air Wing Five (CVW 5) were deployed in support of Operation 'Iraqi Freedom'.

Right: February 1, 2003, an F-14D Tomcat from Fighter Squadron Two (VF-2) – the 'Bounty Hunters' – takes to the air after being launched from the flight deck of the USS *Constellation* (CV 64) during Operation 'Enduring Freedom'.

Below: A flight deck crew member performs a pre-flight check on an F-14A Tomcat aircraft aboard the aircraft carrier USS *Saratoga* (CV 60) during Operation 'Desert Storm'. The Tomcat has been armed with AIM-9 Sidewinder and AIM-54 Phoenix missiles.

ft: Aboard USS *George Washington* (CVN 73), August 19, 2002. Aviation ordnancemen load an M-61A1 20mm Vulcan nnon Gatling gun in an F-14 Tomcat, assigned to the 'Jolly Rogers' of Fighter Squadron One Zero Three (VF-103).

ove: Aviation ordnancemen from the 'Pukin' Dogs' of Fighter Squadron One Four Three (VF-143) unload an AIM-9 ewinder air-to-air short-range missile from an F-14B Tomcat on the flight deck of the USS *John F. Kennedy* (CV 67), April 2002.

low: A F-14 Tomcat assigned to the 'Pukin' Dogs' of Fighter Squadron One Four Three (VF-143) makes its approach for a rrier-arrested landing aboard the USS *John F. Kennedy* (CV 67). Landing a 20 ton aircraft such as the Tomcat requires perb concentration on a moving and often pitching deck. Deck landing at night is particularly stressful. *John F. Kennedy* d her embarked Carrier Air Wing Seven (CVW 7) were conducting combat missions in support of Operation 'Enduring eedom'.

Left: At sea aboard USS *John C. Stennis* (CVN 74), aviation ordnancemen condu[...] planned maintenance on a 20mm Vulca[...] cannon. The Vulcan gun weighs over 250lbs and its ammunition supply of 1,020 rounds plus the feed system weighs another 650lb. It has a six-barrelled rotary action which is externa[...] powered from the aircraft's hydraulic a[...] electrical supply. The most outstanding feature of this weapon is its formidable firepower: 100 rounds fired in just one second, combined with a high muzzle velocity of over 1100 yards per second.

Right: A 58th Tactical Fighter Squadro[...] F-15C Eagle. The aircraft is armed with four AIM-7 Sparrow air-to-air-missiles [...] the fuselage and a mix of two AIM-9 Sidewinders on the left wing and AIM-1[...] AMRAAMs on the right wing.

Opposite page, bottom: Two USAF F-15[...] Eagle fighters of the 33rd Tactical Wing flying in the company of a Royal Saudi F-5E Tiger II fighter aircraft during a mission in support of Operation 'Deser[...] Storm'. The aircraft are armed with AIM[...] Sidewinder and Sparrow air-to-air missiles.

Below: An F-15A Eagle of the 125th Air National Guard, Jacksonville, Florida, launches an AIM-7F/M Sparrow, a radar guided, medium-range, air-to-air missile during a training mission. The Eagle/Sparrow combination had its fine[...] hour during Operation 'Desert Storm', accounting for the greater part of the Coalition's air kills.

p left: Members of the 494th Fighter Squadron, loading the Vulcan gun of an F-15E at Aviano Air Base, Italy, February 23, 96, before flying a combat air patrol over war-torn Bosnia.

ttom left: Missiles sitting on a trailer waiting to be loaded onto a 494th Fighter Squadron F-15 at Aviano Air Base, Italy, oruary 21, 1996. There are four AIM-7 Sidewinders on the top and four AIM-120A AMRAAM air-to air missiles on the ttom shelf. The AMRAAMs have yet to have their fins attached.

ove: The pilot checks one of the AIM-120 AMRAAMs while doing a pre-flight check of his F-15E before flying on a mission support of Operation 'Joint Endeavor' over Bosnia in February 1996. An F-15C destroyed two MiG-29s in one targeting and nch sequence, proving the effectiveness of the AMRAAM missile.

ow: Two 48th Wing, 494th Fighter Squadron F-15Es take-off from Aviano Air Base, Italy, to return to their base at enheath, England, after their missions were completed in the skies over Bosnia, March 4, 1996.

Above: Three F-15Cs and one two-seater F-15D (foremost) aircraft from the 44th and 67th Fighter Squadrons, 18th Wing. The F-15 has a top speed of Mach 2.5 (1,500mph), a service ceiling of 60,000ft, and a combat radius of over 1,000 miles, a truly formidable fighter plane even though the design dates back over 30 years.

Right: An F-15C Eagle, supporting Operation 'Southern Watch', waits on October 27, 2000, for the boom of a KC-135 Stratotanker over Saudi Arabia. The F-15s formed a part of the Coalition forces of the 363d Air Expeditionary Wing that enforced the No-Fly and No-Drive Zone in Southern Iraq to protect and defend against Iraqi aggression.

Below: An F-15A Eagle of the 110th Fighter Squadron, 131st Fighter Wing, Air National Guard, launches an AIM-7 Sparrow missile during a Weapons System Evaluation Program. The AIM-7 Sparrow is a radar-guided, air-to-air missile with a high-explosive warhead.The F-15's superior maneuverability and acceleration are achieved through high engine thrust-to-weight ratio and low wing loading. Low wing-loading is the ratio of aircraft weight to its wing area, and is a vital factor in maneuverability and when combined with the aircraft's high thrust-to-weight ratio enables it to turn tightly without losing airspeed.

Above: An F-15C Eagle of the 19th Fighter Squadron, Elmendorf AFB, Alaska, fires an AIM-120C AMRAAM (Advanced Medium Range Air-to-Air Missile).

Below: A fully armed F-15 Eagle from the Massachusetts Air National Guard's 102nd Fighter Wing flies a combat air patrol mission over New York City in support of Operation 'Noble Eagle'. It is armed with a mix of four medium range AMRAAM missiles and four short range Sidewinders.

Top right: An F-15C Eagle from the 48th Fighter Wing breaks away from a 100th Air Expeditionary Wing KC-135R Stratotanker out of RAF Mildenhall, UK. Armed with AIM-7 Sparrows on the fuselage, AIM-9 Sidewinders on the inboard wing pylon, and Advanced Medium Range Air-to-Air Missiles on the outboard wing pylon, the Eagles were flying Combat Air Patrol missions to maintain air superiority and protect aircraft in NATO Operation 'Allied Force'.

Bottom right: The finely contoured lines of an F-15C are clearly visible in this close-up rear view.

Above left: Base personnel stand by as a 58th Tactical Fighter Squadron F-15D Eagle prepares to fly to Saudi Arabia during Operation 'Desert Shield'.

Left: F-15C Eagle fighters of the 58th Tactical Fighter Squadron about to take off and fly to Saudi Arabia during Operation 'Desert Shield'.

Above: A fully armed 1st Tactical fighter Wing F-15D Eagle sits in its revetment during Operation 'Desert Shield'. Note the Patriot surface-to-air missile launchers deployed in the background.

opposite page: An F-15E pilot assigned to the 494th Fighter Squadron, RAF Lakenheath, England, inspects an AIM-120 missile, April 28, 1999 while doing his pre-sortie walk around. The pylon also carries a fuel tank and an AIM-9 Sidewinder missile. Members of the 494th FS were deployed to Aviano AB, Italy, supporting the NATO Operation 'Allied Force'.

above: Two Air-Defense Fighter F-16A Fighting Falcons from the North Dakota Air National Guard's 178th Fighter Squadron and an F-15C Eagle from the 27th Fighter Squadron in formation during a combat air patrol mission in support of Operation 'Noble Eagle'. The majority of Air National Guard and Air Force Reserve squadrons began patrolling the American skies after the September 11 attack.

Right: A KC-135R Stratotanker refuels an F-16C fighter from the 614th Tactical Fighter Squadron Squadron, 401st Tactical Fighter Wing. Two other F-16s of the 614th TFS fly alongside during Operation 'Desert Shield'. Each F-16 is armed with a pair of AIM-9 Sidewinders.

Below: A Sidewinder-armed F-16C of the 401st TFW on patrol during Operation Desert Shield. The first aerial kill to be credited to a US F-16 did not occur until after 'Desert Storm', during Operation 'Southern Watch' over Iraq, in 1992, when a MiG-25 was brought down with an AIM-120 AMRAAM missile. Mounted under the fighter's fuselage is an AN/ALQ-131 ECM pod.

Below right: An F-16A of the 354 Fighter Wing armed with a pair of Sidewinders.

posite page top: A ground crewman
ides a 388th Tactical Fighter Wing F-16C
hting Falcon onto a taxiway. The 388th
W deployed to Saudi Arabia for Operation
sert Shield'. Note mounted on the
hter's left outboard wing pylon is an
/ALQ-131 Electronic Countermeasures
M) pod. Also mounted on the side of the
gine intake is a Low Altitude Navigation
rgeting Infrared Night (LANTIRN)
vigation pod.

posite page, bottom: An F-16C of the
4th Tactical Fighter Squadron, 401st
ctical Fighter Wing at the time of 'Desert
ield'. The F-16 has a maximum speed
ove Mach 2 at 40,000ft and a service
ling of over 50,000ft. The F-16C is
wered by a General Electric F110-GE-129
rbofan delivering (with afterburner),
,588lb of thrust.

ght: An F-16 Fighting Falcon armed with
ort range AIM-9 Sidewinder missiles takes
during Operation 'Desert Storm'.

low: A 614th TFS F-16C fighter lands
lowing a mission on the first daylight
ack of 'Desert Storm'. The fighter returns
th two Sidewinders on its starboard wing.

posite page, top: An AIM-7F Sparrow
ng fired by an F-16A. It has been
nched from the starboard wing
ter pylon. Also, the fighter is armed
h Sidewinders on wingtip launchers.

posite page, bottom: A two-seat F-
B launches a heat-seeking Sidewinder.
e Sidewinder is one of the oldest,
st expensive, and most successful
ssiles in the US weapons inventory.

;ht: A crew chief performs a pre-flight
pection on an F-16A Fighting Falcon
craft. She is at present concentrating
the AIM-9 Sidewinder missile
unted on the port wing.

ow: The F-16 is also capable of being
uipped with two pairs of Advanced
ort Range Air-to-Air Missiles
RAAM).

posite page, top left: The pilot's Head Up Display (HUD) is the primary flight instrument of the aircraft, providing the
t with basic flight status, navigational steering, and weapon delivery information, all displayed on the small transparent
een which can be seen on top of the aircraft's instrument panels.

posite page, top right: The four small antennae on the nose of this F-16, just before the canopy, are for Identification
end or Foe (IFF). This is a coded transponder system designed for the identification of friendly aircraft and ground units.

posite page, bottom: An F-16 just prior to take-off. The wingtip pylons carry AIM-120 AMRAAM medium-range air-to-air
siles. Inboard of those are AIM-9 Sidewinders, next to those are AGM-88 HARMs for attacking SAM radar sites, and next
hose, 370-US gallon fuel tanks.

ow: Initially conceived as an unsophisticated lightweight air combat fighter, the F-16 Fighting Falcon has matured into a
e hi-tech multirole combat plane.

Above: An F-16 of the 527th Aggressor Squadron which flew the Fighting Falcon for a short time from 1989 until the unit was disbanded in 1990. The USAF had decided to disestablish all of its training aggressor squadrons as a result of major post-Cold War financial cutbacks. The aircraft is seen here in front of a Hardened Aircraft Shelter (HAS).

Below: Four 125th Squadron F-16s of the Air National Guard from the 138th Fighter Wing. They are equipped for the lightweight fighter role with just two Sidewinders missiles each, attached to their wingtip pylons.

ove: Five F-16s of 79th Fighter adron in August 1. Each aircraft is ed with two RAAMs and two ewinders. They also ry two 370-US on external long-ge fuel tanks.

ht: An F-16 of the 'th Fighter Wing of Air National Guard ed at Atlantic City ernational Airport, v Jersey.

Above: A shark-mouthed F-16 is armed with Sidewinders. A LANTIRN navigational pod is attached just under the engine a intake and behind that an AN/ALQ-131 ECM pod can just be made out.

Opposite page: A 120th Fighter Squadron F-16 of the Colorado Air National Guard painted in a flamboyant tiger skin scheme.

Below: The basic defensive armament of the F-16 consists of the internally-mounted M61A1 rotary cannon and two infra-r Sidewinder missiles on the wingtip rails, as shown here.

Opposite page, top: F-16s of the two squadrons of the 52nd Fighter Wing are shown here being led by the aircraft of the commander of the wing.

Opposite page, bottom: F-16s patrol the skies over Northern Iraq. These four fighters have a veritable arsenal of weapons between them including Sidewinders, AMRAAMs, HARM anti-radar missiles, and laser-guided bombs, plus LANTIRN navigational and ECM pods.

Below: This F-16 is armed with a pair of Sidewinders and two AMRAAMs. A LANTIRN navigational pod is attached just under the engine air intake and behind that is an AN/ALQ-184(V)-2 ECM pod, plus two 370-US gallon external fuel tanks.

Above and below: Aboard the USS *Theodore Roosevelt* (CVN 71), April 12, 1999, flight deck personnel prepare F/A-18C Hornets for catapult launch. The *Theodore Roosevelt* and its airwing were deployed to the Adriatic in support of Operation 'Allied Force'.

Above: A load of AIM-120 air-to-air missiles secured before being transported to an aircraft, Aviano Air Base, Italy, in support of NATO Operation 'Allied Force'. Sidewinder missiles can be seen on the trollies in the background.

Below: Aboard the USS *Theodore Roosevelt* (CVN 71), crew members work together to push an F/A-18C Hornet back into its proper position on the flight deck while on operations over the Adriatic and in the sky over Kosovo and Serbia.

Below: A heavily armed F/A-18 Hornet equipped with eight AIM-120 AMRAAM air-to-air missiles under the wings, plus two attached to the aircraft's fuselage and two Sidewinders on the wingtip rails.

Opposite page, top: Carrier flight personnel prepare an F/A-18C from the 'Knighthawks' (VFA-136) for a mission over Bosnia-Herzegovina, March 4, 1996, during operation 'Decisive Endeavor'. The aircraft carries two Sidewinder air-to-air missiles.

Opposite page, bottom: The F/A-18 is an all-weather aircraft used for air superiority and attack. In its air superiority mode is used primarily for fighter escort and for fleet air defense. During Operation 'Desert Storm', the F/A-18 got its first aerial kills, two Chinese built F-7s (MiG-21s), one kill achieved with a Sparrow missile, the other with a Sidewinder.

Above and below: The F/A-18 is flown by the US Navy and Marine Corps in whose service it replaced both the F-4 Phantom and the A-7 Corsair II. The aircraft quickly proved itself to be an ideal carrier-based warplane, offering both supreme agility and exceptional visibility for the pilot.

ove: At sea aboard USS
n F. Kennedy (CV 67) March
2002, aviation
nancemen assigned to the
ldcats' of Strike Fighter
uadron One Three One
A-131) load an AIM-9M
ewinder air-to-air missile
to an F-18C Hornet in
paration for its next
nbat mission. The *Kennedy*
her embarked Carrier Air
ng Seven (CVW 7) were
ducting combat missions
support of Operation
during Freedom'.

ght: An F/A-18C Hornet
kes a tight turn in full
erburner mode while
ducting a fly-by over USS
nstellation (CV 64) during
ctice for *Constellation's*
coming 'Tiger Cruise'. The
nstellation's Carrier Strike
ce was returning from
ployment in which it
pported Operations
uthern Watch', 'Enduring
edom' and 'Iraqi Freedom'.

Above and opposite page, top: Aviation ordnancemen lift an Advanced, Medium Range, Air-to-Air Missile (AMRAAM) to attach it onto an F/A-18 Hornet aboard USS *Nimitz* (CVN 68).

Left: This M1A1 Vulcan 20mm cannon has been removed from an F/A-18 for routine maintenance by an aviation ordnanceman.

Opposite page, bottom: An aviation ordnanceman performs a weapons inspection on an AIM-9 Sidewinder air-to-air missile mounted on an F/A-18F Super Hornet assigned to the 'Black Aces' of Strike Fighter Squadron Fourty One (VFA-41) aboard USS *Nimitz* (CVN 68). The *Nimitz* Battle Group was deployed in support of Operation 'Iraqi Freedom' in the Spring of 2003.

Above and below: F/A-18 Hornets assigned to the 'Silver Eagles' of Marine Fighter Attack Squadron One Fifteen (VMFA-115) which conducted combat missions over Iraq. They are armed with Sidewinders.

Opposite page, top: An F/A-18 Hornet attached to the Naval Fighter Weapons School (NFWS) is photographed in flight during a training mission. NFWS, more commonly known as 'Topgun', trains fleet aircrew in aerial combat tactics.

Opposite page, bottom: U.S. Navy F/A-18 Hornet fighter aircraft (VFA) assigned to Carrier Air Wing One Seven (CVW 17) fly in formation after launching from the aircraft carrier USS *George Washington* (CVN 73). The squadrons pictured include the VFA-81 'Sunliners' (top), the VFA-83 'Rampagers' (center), and the VFA-34 'Blue Blasters' (bottom). *George Washington* and her battlegroup were on a regularly scheduled deployment conducting missions in support of Operation 'Enduring Freedom'.

Left: An F/A-18 Hornet assigned to Strike Fighter Squadron One Five One (VFA-151) create a shock wave as it breaks the sound barrier in the skies over the Pacific Ocea

Below: Although superficially an enlarged F/A-18C/D, the F/A-18E Super Hornet is a new aircraft of increased tactical capability. Th Super Hornet entered service in 1999.

Opposite page: F/A-18Es are made ready for launch on a carrie flight-deck. These Super Hornets are equipped with Sidewinder missiles their wingtips.

opposite page, top: An F/A-18E Super Hornet fitted with a Shared Reconnaissance Pod (SHARP) under the centreline of the aircraft. The pod was developed by Raytheon for the US Navy, to support advanced day and night all-weather tactical reconnaissance missions.

opposite page, bottom: An F/A-18E Super Hornet, of Carrier Air Wing Fourteen (CVW 14), about to be launched from the deck of USS *Abraham Lincoln* while conducting combat operations in support of Operation 'Iraqi Freedom'.

Above: An F/A-18F Super Hornet assigned to the 'Diamondbacks' of Strike Fighter Squadron One Zero Two (VFA-102) getting airborne from USS *John C. Stennis* (CVN 74) while conducting exercises off the coast of California.

Right: The F/A-18F Super Hornet has a prominent antenna on the forward fuselage. Just in front of the canopy windscreen is the APX-111 Combined Interrogator Transponder (CIT). In front of that is the cannon port and either side of that are the gun gas purging intakes.

Above: Two F/A-18F Super Hornets of the 'Black Aces' of Strike Fighter Squadron Four One (VFA-41), of Carrier Air Wing Eleven (CVW 11) during an in-flight refuelling exercise. At the time the 'Black Aces' were with the USS *Nimitz* (CVN 68) deployed in support of Operation Iraqi Freedom.

Below: While making a landing aboard USS *Nimitz* (CVN 68) another F/A-18F Super Hornet from the 'Black Aces' Strike Fighter Squadron Four One (VFA-41) .

ove and below: The Lockheed-Martin/Boeing F-22 Raptor is the most advanced fighter aircraft in the world, combining a olutionary leap in technology and capability with reduced support requirements and maintenance costs. The F-22's mbination of stealth, integrated avionics, maneuverability and supercruise (supersonic flight without afterburner) will give ptor pilots a first-look, first-shot, first-kill capability against the aircraft of any potential enemy. The Raptor is designed to ovide not only air superiority but also air dominance, winning quickly and decisively with few US and allied casualties. The ptor also has an inherent air-to-ground capability.

Above and below: An AIM-9 Sidewinder missile is successfully launched from an F-22 Raptor during a test launch. This major milestone test evaluated the next-generation fighter's ability to fire an air-to-air missile from an internal weapons ba In its primary air-to-air role, the F-22 will carry six AIM-120C and two AIM-9 missiles.

ove and below: The X-35 (F-35 in service) comes in two variants, one with conventional take-off and landing and the other
th STOVL (Short Take-Off and Vertical Landing). The STOVL variant is for service with the Marine Corps. The aircraft
embles a single-engined, scaled-down F-22. The STOVL version also has a lift fan situated behind the cockpit.

The stealthy, multi-role F-35 is intended to replace USAF F-16s, USN F/A-18s, and the Marine Corps' AV-8s. The carrier-capable model will have a larger area wing and tail and be structurally strengthened for carrier operations.